9.90

INTERIM SITE

W9-AOV-062

904 8291

x534 Ardle.N
Ardley, Neil.
Sound and music /

BL71/1/85

D

ACTION SCIENCE

SOUND AND MUSIC

Neil Ardley

Series consultant: Professor Eric Laithwaite

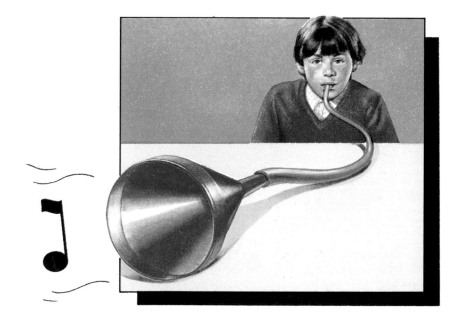

Franklin Watts

London   New York   Toronto   Sydney

EVANSTON PUBLIC LIBRARY
CHILDREN'S DEPARTMENT
1703 ORRINGTON AVENUE
EVANSTON, ILLINOIS 60201

The author
Neil Ardley gained a degree in science and worked as
a research chemist and patent agent before entering
publishing. He is now a full-time writer and is the
author of more than fifty information books on
science, natural history and music.

The consultant
Eric Laithwaite is Professor of Heavy Electrical
Engineering at Imperial College, London. A well-
known television personality and broadcaster, he is
best known for his inventions on linear motors.

© 1984 Franklin Watts Ltd

First published in Great
Britain in 1984 by
Franklin Watts Ltd
12a Golden Square
London W1

First published in the United
States of America by
Franklin Watts Inc.
387 Park Avenue South
New York
N.Y. 10016

Printed in Belgium

UK edition:
ISBN 0 86313 159 X
US edition:
ISBN 0-531-03776-2
Library of Congress
Catalog Card Number:
83-51442

Designed by
David Jefferis

Illustrated by Janos Marffy,
Hayward Art Group and
Arthur Tims

ACTION SCIENCE

SOUND AND MUSIC

Contents

Equipment

In addition to a few everyday items, you will need the following equipment to carry out the activities in this book.

Bottles
Candle
Cardboard tubes (one long, one short)
Funnel
Hosepipe
Loudspeaker
Pan, large
Pencils (two)
Piano
Plastic bag
Plastic bowl

Plastic cup
Record player
Records (unwanted)
Rubber bands
Ruler
Straws
Sugar
Table tennis ball
Thin, strong thread
Tuning fork
Watches (digital and analog)

Introduction

From the moment we speak our first words, sound is very important in our lives. For those of us who are able to hear and to talk, sound is the main way in which we can exchange ideas and information with others. And if, like most people, you are musical or appreciate music, then sound also provides you with a wonderful means of expressing and enjoying yourself.

By doing the activities in this book, you will first understand how sound is made and how it travels to our ears. Then you can discover ways of using sound, as in a phonograph and stethoscope, and try experiments like finding the speed of sound and blowing out a flame just by using sound.

You can also make some very simple musical instruments that show you how sound is produced in music. Even if you are not musical, you should enjoy the sounds that they make.

※ This symbol is used throughout the book. It shows you where to find the scientific explanation for the results of an activity.

You'll hear a sound if something vibrates strongly and quickly.

△ You can feel how the loudspeaker vibrates by very gently touching the inside surface. Get permission to use the loudspeaker in this way, and be very careful not to damage it.

Jumping ball

Move a big loudspeaker connected to a radio or a record or tape player so that it lies on its back. Take the cover off the speaker and gently place a table tennis ball in it. Switch on, turn up the volume and see how the table tennis ball jumps about.

✳ When anything makes a sound, all or part of it vibrates back and forth. The surface inside the loudspeaker vibrates strongly when it makes loud sounds. This vibration is enough to make the ball jump.

6

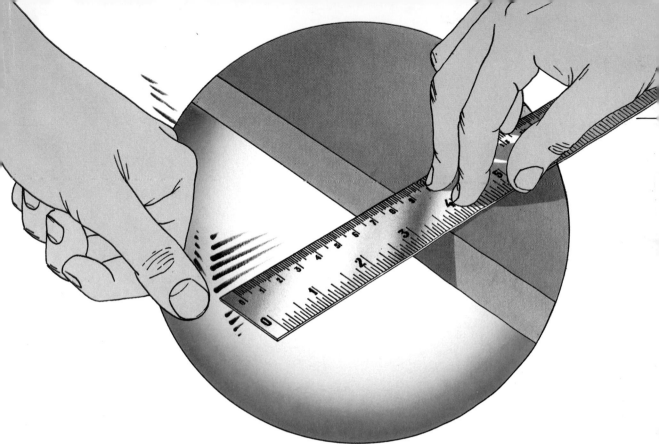

Twanging time

Take a metal or wooden ruler and put it on a table top so that part of it juts over the edge. Press one end firmly to the table and twang the other end. This section of the ruler vibrates and gives out a sound. Make the section shorter or longer. Hear how the sound goes higher or lower in pitch. See too how twanging the ruler harder or softer makes the sound louder or quieter.

✳ When you shorten the vibrating section of the ruler, the vibrations increase in speed. If an object vibrates faster, the sound that it gives rises in pitch. Twanging harder makes the vibration stronger, so the sound is louder.

△ To make a sound, an object has to vibrate quickly — at least twenty times every second.

▽ You can speak and sing because vocal cords in your throat vibrate quickly and strongly. Touch your Adam's apple to feel them at work.

7

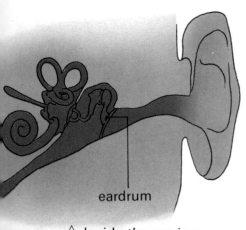

eardrum

△ Inside the ear is a membrane called the eardrum. Like the stretched plastic, it vibrates when sound waves enter the ear. Signals then travel to the brain and we hear the sound.

▽ The plastic bag must be as tight as possible.

How does sound travel to your ears?

Sound waves

Take a bowl and stretch a plastic bag over the top. Fasten it with a rubber band as shown, and sprinkle a few grains of sugar on the plastic. Then take a big pan, hold it near the bowl and strike it with a spoon a few times. The sugar grains jump about whenever the pan gives out a sound.

✹ As the pan vibrates, it makes the air vibrate too. Invisible waves of vibrating air move through the air. These are sound waves. When they strike the plastic, they make it vibrate too. This vibration causes the sugar grains to jump about.

Sound gun

Use a sound gun to extinguish a candle without touching it or blowing it out. Take a cardboard tube and stick two circles of card over the ends. Make a hole about $\frac{3}{8}$ in across in one end. Next light a candle and point the tube toward it with the hole facing the flame. Tap the other end sharply and the candle goes out!

☀ As you tap the card, you produce sound waves which make thc air inside the tube vibrate. When these vibrations reach the hole at the end, a little puff of air travels out and puts the flame out.

△ Choose a candle that does not burn too strongly, or the flame will only flicker instead of going out. Do this experiment in a place without any drafts.

9

Penetrating sounds

Sound can travel more easily through some materials than through the air.

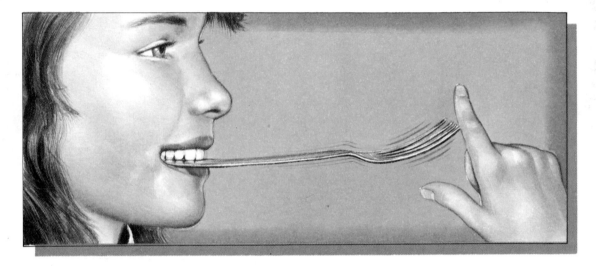

△ Take great care not to hurt your teeth or mouth. For best results, use a fork with long prongs.

Skull sounds

Hold a fork and twang the prongs. You'll hear a faint ping. Now grip it in your back teeth. Twang it again. This time, a loud ringing sound bursts through your head!

✺ The first time, the sound made by the vibrating prongs travels through the air. The second time, it travels along the metal handle and then into your jawbone and skull to reach your ears. Sound travels much more easily through metal and bone than through air. This is why the fork sounds much louder the second time.

Secret message

Send a secret message in a code that uses sounds such as Morse code. Get a friend to put an ear to a wall. Then tap the message quietly on the wall. No one else will hear the tapping sounds, but your friend will receive them clearly some distance away or on the other side of the wall.

✳ Tapping the wall makes it vibrate slightly. The vibrations are not strong enough to give much sound in the air. But they produce sound waves that travel quickly and easily through the material in the wall. Pressing an ear to the wall enables the waves to reach the ear and be heard.

▽ Sound moves easily through brick, stone and glass. This is why sounds such as birds singing can come through walls and windows from outside.

11

Transmission of sound

Punch a hole in the base.

△ Stick tape over any jagged edges on the cans. Fix the thread by pushing it through the hole in each can and then knotting it so that it does not come out.

Why does sound move through some things and not others?

Tin can telegraph
Take two empty tin cans and remove the lids. Wash out the cans and make a small hole in the base of each one. Then fix a long piece of thin but strong thread between the cans. Two people should hold the cans with the thread stretched tight. One person then places his or her can to an ear while the other person speaks quietly into the other can. The voice will be heard clearly in the first can. Now let the string go slack – the voice cannot be heard.

✹ Speaking produces sound waves, and these travel into the can and along the tight string to the other can. This is because a tight string can itself vibrate and carry the sound waves. A slack string cannot vibrate and will not carry sound.

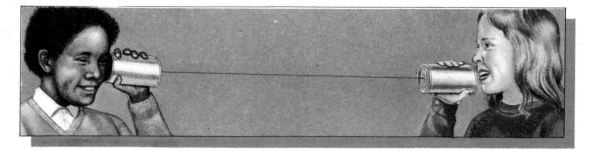

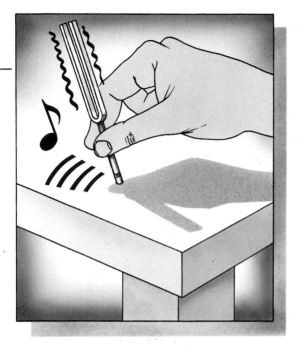

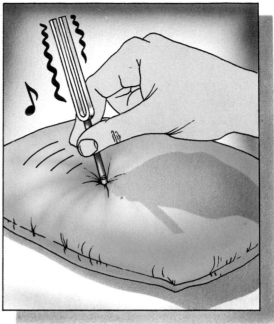

Sound tester

Take a tuning fork. Make it sound by striking the prongs on a hard object and then placing the base on various materials. Try metal, wood, plastic objects, a towel, a cushion, books, fruit, rubber, cork and so on, and also water. Only hard materials give a good sound. Soft objects and liquids soak up the sound of the fork.

A tuning fork sounds loud when it sets a surface vibrating strongly. In fact most of the sound you hear comes from the vibrating surface on which the fork is placed. Hard materials produce a loud sound because they can vibrate too. Little vibration gets through the soft materials or water, so the sound is much quieter.

▽ Vibrations do not pass easily through air. In thermal windows, a thick layer of air between two panes of glass stops strong vibrations getting to the inner pane. This prevents sound entering the room from outside.

Making sound louder

△ Instruments like the violin are built so that the whole body of the instrument vibrates when the strings are played. This makes the sound of the strings much louder.

▽ Use a record that you no longer want for this experiment as the pin may damage the grooves.

Here are two different ways of increasing the loudness of soft sounds.

Primitive phonograph

Take a plastic cup and stick a pin into its base. Then hold the cup lightly in one hand over a record spinning on a record player. Lower the pin gently on to the record, and you'll hear the music coming from the cup!

✸ As the pin settles in the groove on the record, it vibrates and gives out a weak sound. The vibrations pass along the pin to the plastic cup. The whole cup now vibrates and therefore makes the sound of the music much louder. Early record players or phonographs worked in this way.

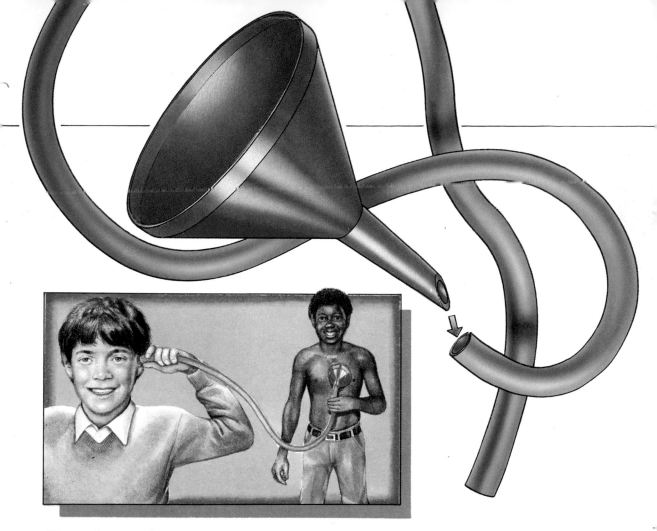

Simple stethoscope

Take a piece of plastic tube or rubber hosepipe about a yard long and stick a funnel into one end. Ask a friend to place the funnel on his or her chest while you hold the end of the tube close to your ear. You'll hear your friend's heart beating.

✳ The funnel picks up the weak sound of the heartbeat. The sound waves then squeeze into the tube and reach the ear. Forcing sound waves into a narrow space like this makes the sound louder.

△ This instrument is like the stethoscope that a doctor uses to listen to your heartbeat. The doctor's stethoscope has two tubes, one for each ear. The heartbeat has a low, thumping sound.

High and low sounds

Why are some sounds higher or lower in pitch than others?

△ Use an old record for this experiment as it may be damaged when you change the speed.

Strange voices

Play a record of a singer and alter the speed of the record player. Switch the player off then on again, or use your finger as shown. As the record slows down, the singer's voice gets lower. Speed up the record, and the voice gets higher.

✹ The needle of the record player vibrates as the wiggly groove in the record moves past it. If the record speeds up, the needle vibrates more quickly. This makes the voice sound higher in pitch. If the record slows down, fewer vibrations occur and the pitch drops.

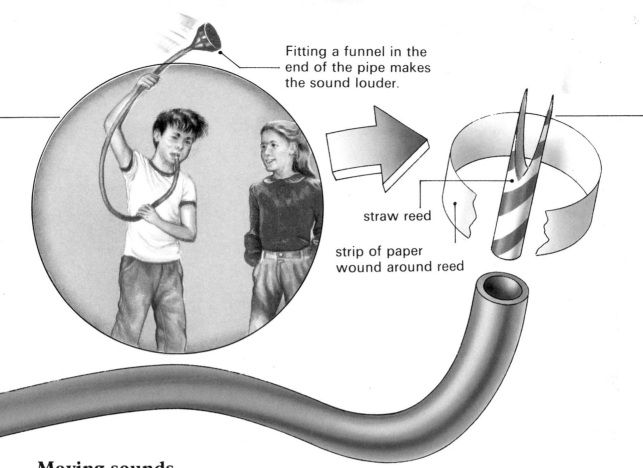

Fitting a funnel in the end of the pipe makes the sound louder.

straw reed

strip of paper wound around reed

Moving sounds

Make a straw reed as described on page 25. Wind some paper around it so that it fits tightly into the end of a long piece of hosepipe. Fix a funnel into the other end of the pipe. Blow into the straw to make a note. As you blow, whirl the pipe and hear how the note goes up and down in pitch.

✳ As the end of the pipe moves toward you, more sound waves reach your ear in every second than when it is moving away. Your eardrum vibrates more quickly, and the sound rises in pitch. As the pipe moves away, the vibrations get slower and the pitch falls.

▽ This change in sound is called the Doppler effect. You can also hear it when a vehicle with a wailing siren such as a fire engine passes.

Sound reflections

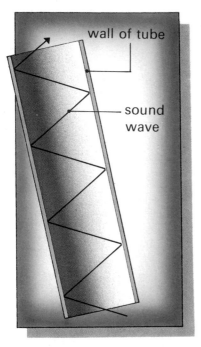

wall of tube

sound wave

▽ If you do not have a ticking watch, quietly rub two fingernails together instead.

Sound is reflected from things just as light is reflected from mirrors.

Sound tube

Take a long cardboard tube or make one from a big sheet of paper. Hold a ticking watch at arm's length so that it cannot be heard. Now put the tube between the watch and your ear.

✸ Sound waves normally spread out in all directions, making the sound weaker with distance. But sound waves from the watch enter the tube and are reflected by its walls. They bounce from side to side until they reach your ear. Because the sound waves cannot leave the tube, the sound is as strong at your ear as it is by the watch.

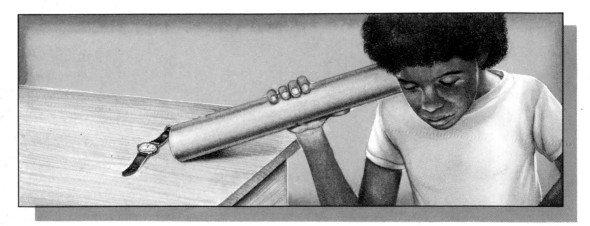

Simple amplifier

Listen to a constant sound, such as music from a radio or record player. Now cup your hands around your ears. The music sounds louder. Take your hands away, and the music is softer again.

※ As you listen to the music, most of the sound waves go past your head and miss your ears. When you cup your hands around your ears, the curved surfaces of your hands reflect a greater number of sound waves into your ears. Because your ears receive more sound waves, the sound is amplified, or increased, and it grows louder.

▽ Bats find their way in the dark by listening to the sounds of high-pitched squeaks bouncing off objects. Their large ears help to amplify these sounds.

The speed of sound

Sound waves move very quickly, but you can detect their motion.

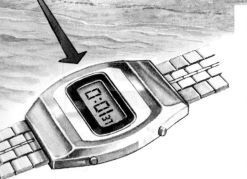

OH!

OH!

△ Find the distance by walking to the wall or cliff with a steady pace. Count the paces. Then measure your pace and multiply it by the number of paces.

Echo time

Stand at least 600 ft away from a high wall or cliff. Give a loud, very short shout. You will hear an echo. Using a digital stop watch, time how long it takes to hear the echo. Then measure the distance to the wall or cliff. Multiply the distance by 2 and divide it by the time. This is the speed of sound in feet per second.

※ You hear the echo because it takes a short time for the sound to reach the wall or cliff and then to be reflected back to your ears. The speed of sound is the total distance that a sound travels divided by the time it takes.

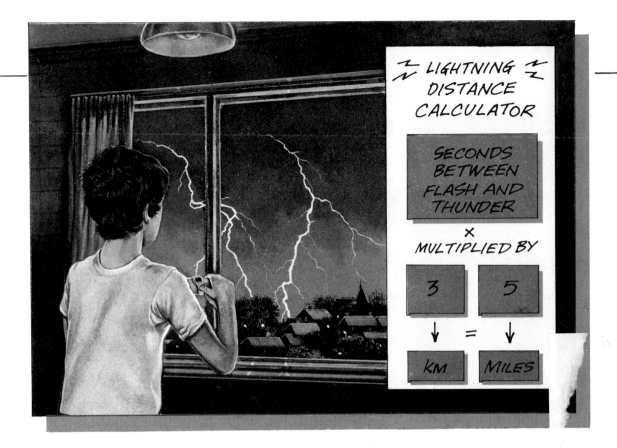

Lightning Distance Calculator

SECONDS BETWEEN FLASH AND THUNDER

× MULTIPLIED BY

3   5

↓ = ↓

KM   MILES

How far away is lightning?

Find out how far away lightning strikes in a storm. As soon as you see a flash, begin counting or timing in seconds. Stop as soon as you hear the thunder. Multiply the time by five. The result is the distance of the lightning in miles.

✹ The light of the flash travels to you in a tiny fraction of a second. The roar of the thunder takes time because it moves at the speed of sound. As this speed is about 1,000 feet per second, it takes 5 seconds for the thunder to travel every mile.

△ Lightning causes thunder because the flash is extremely hot. The air expands violently in the path of the flash, producing strong sound waves that are heard as thunder.

21

Find out how one sound can produce another sound.

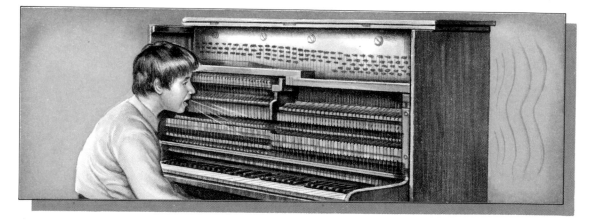

△ The sustaining pedal is the one on the right. It is often called the loud pedal. It doesn't actually make the sound of the piano louder. It allows the strings to continue to vibrate, so that the notes last longer. Your voice echoes in the piano because the sound it produces takes time to die away.

Piano echoes

Open a piano and stand in front of it, pressing down the sustaining pedal. Face the strings and shout or sing something loudly. You'll then hear the sound of your voice echoing from the piano!

✳ When you make a sound, you produce various high or low notes. Pressing the pedal allows all the strings in the piano to vibrate. When the sound waves of your voice strike the strings, they set some vibrating. The strings with the same notes as those in your voice start to vibrate. They give these notes, and the piano produces the sound of your voice like an echo.

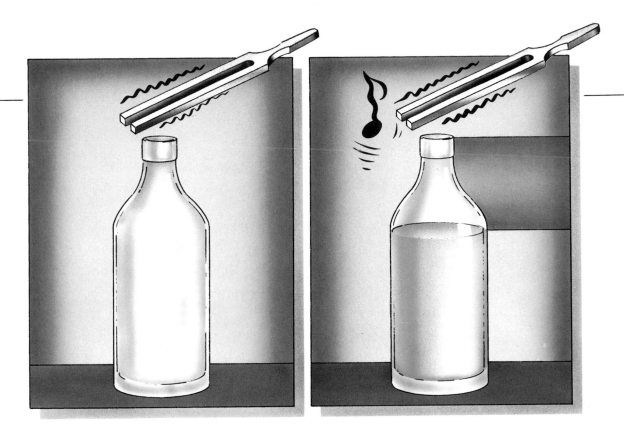

Singing bottle

Sound a tuning fork by striking it and hold the prongs over the neck of an empty bottle. You'll probably hear only a weak note coming from the prongs. Now put some water in the bottle and try again. At a certain level, the bottle will sing loudly with the note of the fork.

The air in the bottle can vibrate to produce a sound. The pitch depends on the amount of air inside. Filling the bottle with water raises the pitch. When the bottle's note is at the same pitch as the tuning fork, the prongs set the air vibrating too and the bottle sounds the note.

△ Blowing across the top of the bottle will enable you to hear the pitch of the bottle's note. You can then add water until the bottle is in tune with the fork.

This effect, in which sound at a particular pitch causes things to produce the same pitch, is called resonance. It is important in making musical instruments and designing concert halls.

Musical sounds

Make some simple instruments to find out how musical instruments work.

Stretched strings

Take a piece of thin but strong thread about a yard long. Attach one end to a table leg and the other to a carton. Then lay the string over two pencils on the table top as shown. Put some marbles or other weights in the carton to stretch the string. Pluck the string to give a note. Move the pencils or change the weights to get different notes.

☀ The note of a stretched string gets higher if the part of the string that vibrates is shortened, and if the pull on the string is greater. The guitar, violin, cello and piano all have stretched strings.

▽ Place paper under the pencils. Mark the positions of both pencils, then move one to get different notes. Mark the pencil positions that give notes of the scale. You can then move the pencil to these marks to play a tune.

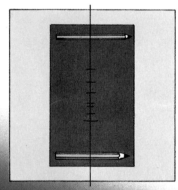

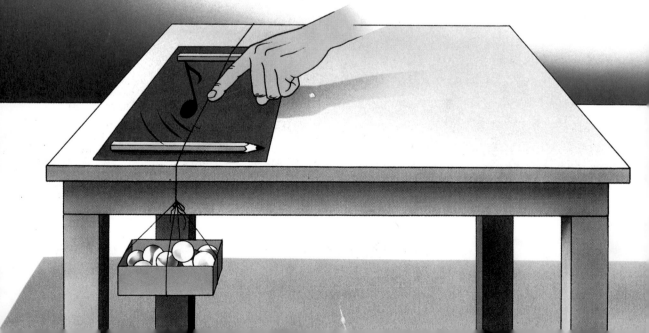

Reed pipes

Take a straw and cut the end into a V-shape as shown. Press the two halves of the end together so that they almost touch. Place this end in your mouth and blow hard. Out comes a loud, harsh note. Shorten the straw to get a higher note.

✺ As you blow, the two halves of the reed vibrate. They set the air in the straw vibrating and it makes a sound. If the length of vibrating air is shorter, the note produced is higher. Woodwind instruments that contain reeds, such as the clarinet, oboe, bassoon and saxophone, work in this way.

△ Make two or more of these reed pipes in different lengths. Put them all in your mouth and blow hard. Adjust the lengths to change the sound.

Continued overleaf

25

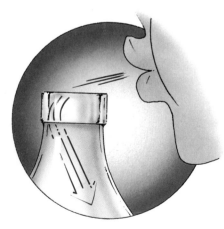

▽ To get each bottle to sound, you have to purse your lips, place them by the top of the neck and gently blow down into it.

Bottle organ

Take several bottles, if possible of the same size. Fill one half-full of water and blow across the top to get a note from it. Fill the others with different amounts of water to get notes of the scale. You can then play simple tunes on the bottles.

☀ Blowing across the top of the bottle makes the air inside vibrate. The flute produces a sound in the same way. The pitch of the note depends on the amount of air inside and therefore on the level of the water. An organ contains pipes of different lengths that make separate notes like this.

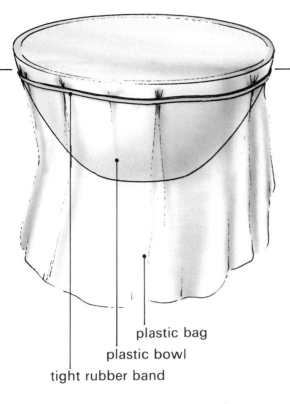

plastic bag
plastic bowl
tight rubber band

Toy timpani

Take a plastic bowl and stretch a plastic bag tightly over it. Fix a rubber band around the rim of the bowl. Hold the bowl as shown and tap the rim; it should sound like a drum. Tap it more times, squeezing the bag to make the plastic tighter and looser. The note of the drum rises and falls.

△ To get a good sound, the plastic must be stretched smoothly without any wrinkles.

✳ A drum makes a sound because the skin across the drum vibrates when it is struck. If the skin is stretched tighter, it vibrates faster and the note of the drum gets higher. Timpani or kettledrums may have screws or a pedal to tighten the skin and change the note.

Continued *overleaf*

Hosepipe horn

Take the stethoscope shown on page 17, and place the end of the pipe over your lips. Press your lips tightly together and force air between them. You should be able to get several notes from the pipe. Using the mouthpiece of a brass instrument will help.

▽ The pipe can be made to produce several different notes, called harmonics, just by lip pressure. To get more notes, the length of the vibrating air has to be made longer or shorter. In most brass instruments, the length of tubing can be changed to do this. The funnel helps to project the sound forward like the bell on a real instrument.

The vibration of your lips sets the air in the pipe vibrating, and produces a note. As you tighten or slacken your lips, the vibration gets faster or slower and you can sound a few other notes. Brass instruments such as the trumpet, trombone and horn make sounds in this way.

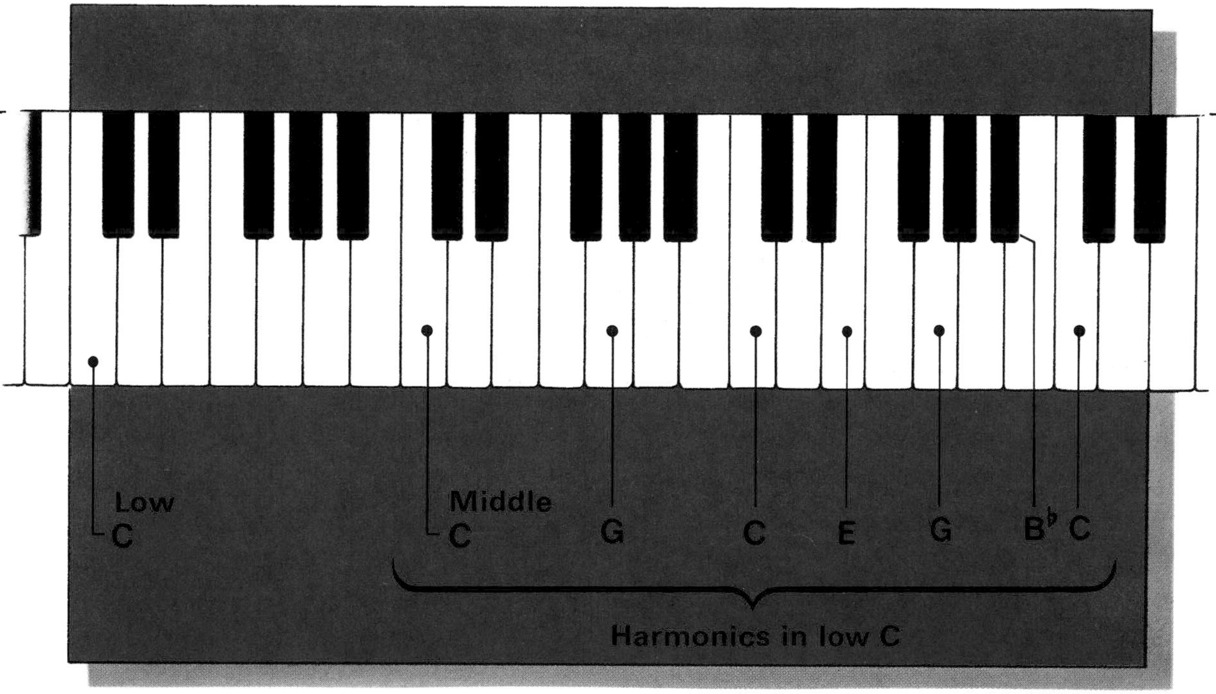

Unheard sounds

Sit at the piano and gently press down middle C so the note does not sound. Keep the key pressed and strike the C an octave below with a short but hard blow. As the low note stops, middle C can be heard ringing even though it has not been played! Try finding other notes that ring like this after sounding a low C first. Only a few notes will do so.

△ If you know the names of the notes, you should find harmonics at middle C, then (going higher) G, C, E, G, B flat and C again. No other notes should ring if the piano is in tune. Find the harmonics in other notes in this way.

When the low key is struck, the sound produced contains a mixture of higher notes called harmonics. Normally these notes cannot be heard separately. Operating the piano keys in this way picks out the harmonics in the low sound.

More about sound

Brass instruments
A brass player can get a set of notes from an instrument just by using the lips alone. This is because the lips can make the air vibrate faster or slower inside the instrument. But the tubing of most brass instruments can also be made longer or shorter by pressing valves or moving a slide. This changes the set of notes made by the lips. A brass player gets notes by changing the lip pressure and by operating the valves or the slide, often at the same time.

Percussion instruments
These are instruments like drums and cymbals which usually make noises rather than notes. The player hits the body of the instrument to make it vibrate and produce a sound. Some percussion instruments, like the xylophone and timpani, can gives notes with a definite pitch.

Pitch
A note with a high pitch sounds high, like the notes toward the right-hand side of the piano keyboard. Notes that are low in pitch sound deep, like the notes to the left-hand side of the keyboard. The pitch is actually the number of vibrations that occur every second in a sound.

Sound waves
A sound wave is produced by a surface that vibrates (moves back and forth) quickly. As the surface vibrates, it disturbs the air around it. Bands of high and low pressure move out through the air. These are sound waves. Sound waves can also move through liquids and hard solids in a similar way.

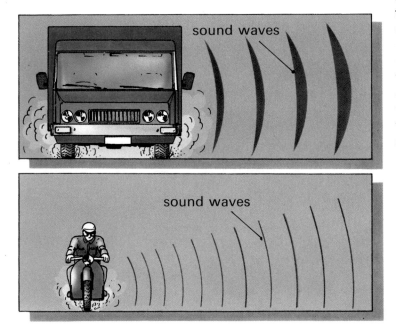

sound waves

sound waves

◁ A truck gives a loud and deep sound; its sound waves are strong and far apart. A scooter is less loud and higher in pitch; its sound waves are weaker and closer together.

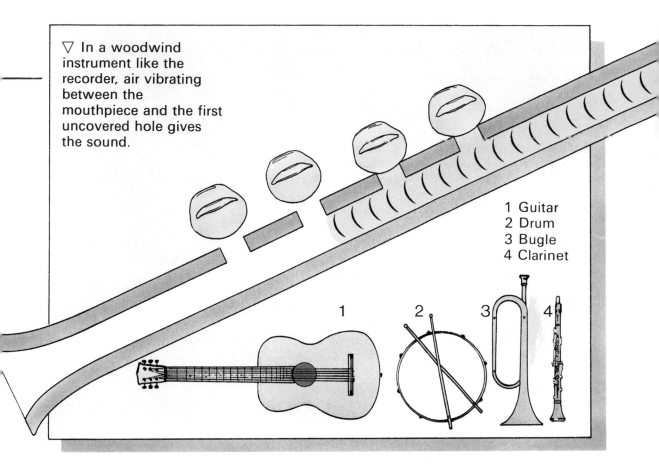

▽ In a woodwind instrument like the recorder, air vibrating between the mouthpiece and the first uncovered hole gives the sound.

1 Guitar
2 Drum
3 Bugle
4 Clarinet

String instruments
These instruments have stretched strings that vibrate to give sounds. The strings can be plucked, hit or bowed. The pitch of the note depends on the length of the string, its thickness and how tightly it is stretched. The length of the vibrating part of a string may be altered with the fingers. In this way, guitarists, violinists and cellists get many notes from a few strings.

Voice
When we make a sound, we set the vocal cords in the throat vibrating. The cords are tight bands that vibrate as air passes over them. Muscles can alter the tightness of the vocal cords to give different notes. However, women have higher voices than men because their vocal cords are shorter. We can also change the shape of the mouth and use the tongue and teeth to give different sounds.

△ The four families of musical instruments: strings (1), percussion (2), brass (3) and woodwind (4).

Woodwind instruments
All these instruments have holes along the side. The player gets different notes by covering and uncovering the holes. The air is set vibrating by the player blowing into a mouthpiece at the top of the instrument.

Index